Christmas Story in Paris

# Christmas Story in Paris

## by Luckner M. Pierre

theme: To acknowledge the sharing value of Christmas that preserves the human spirit of sharing in the heart of Santa Claus

"Courage is the most important of all the virtues, because without courage you can't practice any other virtue consistently. You can practice any virtue erratically, but nothing consistently without courage."

- Stedman Graham

Christmas Story in Paris                    Luckner M. Pierre

Copyright © 2020 Luckner M. Pierre. All rights reserved.

This book or any portion thereof may not be
Reproduced or used in any manner without written permission except for the
Use of brief quotations in a book review.
It may not be re-sold or given away to other people.
If you would like to share this book with another person,
Please purchase an additional copy for each recipient.
Thank you for respecting the hard work of this author.

No part of this book may be reproduced, stored in a retrieval system, or
Transmitted by any means without the written permission of the author.

Cover design by Amazon

Published by Amazon on 12/10/2020

**ISBN #: 9798695999976**

**Christmas Story in Paris**           Luckner M. Pierre

"I rather witness a growing appreciation from people than experience the absence of appreciation at the end."
- Mr. Pierre

Christmas Story in Paris                    Luckner M. Pierre

"Don't cry because of what you lost,
Smile because of what you learned."

- Personal Motto

Christmas Story in Paris                    Luckner M. Pierre

*Dedicated to the heart of Christmas in the international community*

**Christmas Story in Paris**     **Luckner M. Pierre**

"Meeting new people at the right place
at the right time creates meaningful journeys that
brings Christmas transformation forever."
- Mr. Pierre

Christmas Story in Paris                      Luckner M. Pierre

> "Where there is hope there is life,
> where there is life there is possibility,
> and where there is possibility change can occur."
> - Jesse Jackson

> "Nourish your hopes, but do not overlook realities."
> - Winston Churchill

Christmas Story in Paris                                    Luckner M. Pierre

"We make a living by what we get, but we make a life by what we give."
- Winston Churchill



"Studies show that volunteering can improve and maintain your mental and physical health, as well as helping with the effects of stress, anxiety and low self-esteem."
- Volunteer Centre Camden

Christmas Story in Paris          Luckner M. Pierre

## CONTENTS

Acknowledgements

Introduction: Joyful Smiles

Christmas Story in Paris                1

<u>Short Articles</u>

Internal Anxiety                        6

Timid or Courageous                     7

Mr. International                       9

Well-being Needs True Happiness         11

<u>Poems of Encouragement</u>

Poem: Christmas Loves Children          13

Poem: Gratitude of Christmas            14

Poem: Irrepressible Generosity          15

Poem: Life of a Volunteer               16

Author's BIO                            17

About the Author                        20

## Acknowledgements

Thanks to the heart of Paris where I first gained Santa Claus experience for giving me an opportunity to share my writing journey with all volunteers in the Paris community.

Thanks to Amazon for self-publishing this Christmas book.

Thanks to the French Salvation Army where I practice my French Christmas story like the voice of encouragement.

Thanks to all the Paris shopping stores that promote and preserve the spirit of Christmas on a regular basis in the Christmas season.

Thanks to Judy Nicault. Thanks to Diana Baranoff. Thanks to Vida Quartey. Thanks all the volunteers at the Christmas Market aka Marché de Noël.

Thanks to Sensi Armando for his generosity to my teenage life. Thanks to Tammy Mesdaieu and to my aunts for their generosity. Thanks to Francis Ansong for his generosity to my future.

Thanks to every reader for taking the time to read this short book that will guide the human conscious through the breath of love.

I am proud to be Santa Claus for as long as fifty years or more.

Christmas is my hero even if the temperature is zero. Christmas is here, there and in the air without despair.

Happy Christmas and Happy Reading,
Mr. Luckner Pierre

Christmas Story in Paris                    Luckner M. Pierre

## Introduction: Joyful Smiles

"I rather witness a growing appreciation from people than experience the absence of appreciation at the end."
- Mr. Pierre

Writing this Christmas book has been very pleasant and nurturing as it nurtures my inner well-being.

Christmas is a time where people want presents, yet some forget to acknowledge the sharing value of Christmas that clearly understands the therapy of Christmas.

In November 2017 and 2018, I committed myself to the role of Father Christmas even though it was and still is the "lowest paid salary" for six weeks of sitting in the grotto. The low salary did not bother me because Father Christmas or Santa Claus became my favourite seasonal job in the world. However, at that time, I needed to read the real Christmas story again because the last time I read the Christmas story was when I was a teenager in Miami.

On the other hand, my love for being Father Christmas is greater than any other job I worked in the past.

While the global restrictions against the coronavirus remain stable throughout 2020, the tradition of Christmas should still be celebrated and enjoyable in December 2020.

Christmas Story in Paris          Luckner M. Pierre

Before and after the Christmas season, the intensity of stress or tension upon the world leaves most people psychologically imbalanced, which can be healed by Christmas therapy.

Throughout every season, I like to listen to traditional Christmas songs that reminds me of the sharing value of Christmas as it also speaks to my conscious pleasantly.

Whether it be Valentine's Day, Mother's day or Halloween day,
I like to be in the Christmas mood like Christmas hypnosis, which is healthy for my social well-being. The positive force of Christmas is a healthy-feeling for internal healing and also for global healing. If some people choose not to appreciate my writing journey in Camden, at least the heart of Christmas appreciates my writing journey forever. Christmas is my hero even if the temperature is zero. Twenty or thirty years later, I still see myself being Father Christmas even if the salary might be lower than today or as a volunteer.

Indeed, my sincere appreciation for Christmas is far greater and wider than the immeasurable sky.

Christmas Story in Paris                    Luckner M. Pierre

In other seasons throughout the year, I profoundly reflect on the sharing value of Christmas like sleepless nights because the thought of Christmas always puts me in a positive mood like food for thought.

From hot chocolate with whip cream, to cinnamon chai tea, to a lovely Latte with brown sugar, Christmas is here, there and in the air without despair.

On YouTube on my smartphone, I like to listen to traditional Christmas songs even before Christmas season.

Understanding Christmas is the best day of my life and understanding that Christmas is always an unforgettable experience that refreshes my well-being and perspective on life is remarkable and a lifestyle. I love Christmas, and Christmas loves me with a sense of social enjoyment and day-filled satisfaction forever.

Money cannot buy true happiness, yet the joy of Christmas is my true happiness. Ho, Ho, Ho, Happy Christmas to all.

Happy Reading,
Mr. Pierre

Christmas Story in Paris                    Luckner M. Pierre

### Christmas Story in Paris

"Meeting new people at the right place
at the right time creates meaningful journeys that
brings Christmas transformation forever."
- Mr. Pierre

On the morning of Christmas Eve at 6am, the greatness of Father Christmas prepares to deliver the most anticipated Christmas book in the London community through the transformation of Christmas.

In the North Pole, the reindeers eat their carrots while Father Christmas eats chocolate chip pancakes and waffles with fat-free syrup and peanut butter cake, cinnamon coffee and raspberry lemonade and then feels like a jack rabbit. At 7am, children and adults continue to stare at the Christmas tree in hope of receiving a present earlier than expected and are hypnotise by the magic of Christmas as their eyes stare at the Christmas lights on the tree from left to right on every night. Throughout the day, radio stations play traditional Christmas songs and all car and lorry drivers listen to the melody of a Christmas playlist that lingers in their conscious like the voice of encouragement.

Christmas Story in Paris　　　　　　　　　Luckner M. Pierre

In the grotto, candy toys and magical toys for girls and boys stare in every space of air waiting to share the fairness of Christmas. On his Christmas list, Father Christmas has more than one million names to serve like a flying bird that is heard in every herd and like a new Christmas word.

Returning in the grotto, one of the boys kindly give a letter and chocolate cookies to Father Christmas altruistically.

After serving at least one thousand children in the grotto, Father Christmas is still eager and energetic to preserve the spirit of Christmas like one million years.

On Christmas day, all Londoners are awaken like a breakfast banana shake and are ready to eat more Christmas cakes.

After 8am, all Londoners receive the gift of a lifetime in a Christmas story book underneath the Christmas tree that brings people together in the coldest weather like finding new treasure.

As Sam, who is seven, and Rachael, who is nine, walk into the grotto on the theme of circus clowns and they see Father Christmas who says, "Ho, Ho, Ho, and Happy Christmas!"

Christmas Story in Paris                    Luckner M. Pierre

"Have you been a good boy and good girl this year?" Sam says, "I am always good at school, and I finished all my homework assignments on time." Father Christmas speaks to Rachael, "Have you been a good girl this year?" Rachael says, "I have maintained good grades in school and I love to act cool."

Father Christmas says, "That's great and awesome. I am proud of both of you. Good conduct and good grades in school are equally important. Father Christmas says, "That's great and awesome. I am proud of both of you. I expect all of you to maintain good conduct and good grades every year. Here is a lovely present for you and a lovely present for you. Have a great time at home and always respect the rules in the house. I will see you on Christmas day. Ho, Ho, Ho, Happy Christmas.

As the electricity of Christmas lights burn electrical calories, every Londoner receives an energy-saving solution that reduces the household electricity with simplicity. On the magical day of Christmas, the satisfaction of London begins to grow and feels twenty years younger without the emotion of hunger. In the

Christmas Story in Paris					Luckner M. Pierre

outdoor environment, smartphone and iPhone users take a lovely photo of Father Christmas and Father Christmas walks around for five to six hours to encourage everyone like no tomorrow and no sorrow like empathy-learning.

Returning to the grotto, every boy and girl receives a Christmas poem and this encouraging poem fulfils the heart of Christmas. Christmas candies on the tree grab the eyes by surprise. In December, every night feels like Christmas day even though it's the first week of December like Christmas insomnia that develops cheerful habits for other seasons throughout the year like less hysteria and more humility where Christmas smiles run many miles.

The reminder to all Londoners is the gift of Christmas is not about Father Christmas, the gift of Christmas is about serving others like sisters and brothers.

Christmas day in 2020 became a new breakthrough that re-news the tradition of Christmas here, there and in the air and without despair. With a new perception of this particular Christmas

**Christmas Story in Paris**　　　　　　　　Luckner M. Pierre

experience, all Londoners became more productive and proficient in other areas of the human life effectively.

Many thanks to Father Christmas for re-newing and rebuilding the tradition of Christmas like stretching the human imagination to another planet like the sociology of Christmas of Christmas therapy.

**Christmas Story in Paris**　　　　　　　　　**Luckner M. Pierre**

### Internal Anxiety

*"To win against anxiety, one must be intuitively aware of the internal battle that is not seen by the human eye."*
*- Mr. Pierre*

Internal anxiety sometimes worries me, so I burn at least three thousand calories of intense cardio at the gym on a weekly basis. Perhaps when my body feels tension it sends a non-verbal message to my brain like the mind-body reaction in fractions. When I have a migraine attack, I quickly commute to the gym and cardio exercise makes me feel migraine-free. Anxiety displays itself even in my interpersonal communication skills that needs to heal like swallowing a pill.

My confidence combats against anxiety all the time and wins the invisible battle. Anxiety comes and anxiety goes and sometimes it is re-activated, so I rely on cardio exercise and weight-lifting as the safest method for my intellectual journey. Overall, internal anxiety is just as significant as external anxiety to ensure the tension of the muscle vanishes like smoke in the air on all levels of life. I love to feel anxiety-free and stress-free like the scenery of the beach environment that nurtures my skin and then I begin to win.

**Christmas Story in Paris**                      **Luckner M. Pierre**

## Timid or Courageous

> "Courage is the most important of all the virtues, because without courage you can't practice any other virtue consistently. You can practice any virtue erratically, but nothing consistently without courage."
> - Stedman Graham."

The emotion of timidity creates inner fear against the human body that needs the washing of fearless water like vinegar and hot water. Before I became a rapper as a hobby, I used to be timid until I jumped off the stage for my individual stage performance in 1999.

If I was shorter than I am, the heart of courage still lives in me like positive adjectives spinning in my brain. Long-term timidity could sometimes lead to judgmental thoughts that need the anchor of courage and the belt of bravery. The thoughts of courage lead to encouragement as it encourages people to encourage others endlessly. When people demonstrate fault-finding intentions against me, the boldness of my courageous heart prove to be reliable, stable and relentless.

I will never let anyone devalue nor discourage my meaningful journey because my self-worth is very special to me. Never be timid to people nor to yourself. Let the boldness of courage supersede your heart and character like fruits and vegetables healthy for a new way of thinking

**Christmas Story in Paris**                        **Luckner M. Pierre**

and a new way of feeling through emotional resiliency like the courage of the earth fearlessly.

**Christmas Story in Paris**                          **Luckner M. Pierre**

## Mr. International

> "Music is the universal language
> that connects me to the world."
> - Tania León

Crossing borders is an unforgettable experience that exercises the muscle of human flexibility. For example, Pitbull, a Miami-based rapper, is a perfect example of what it means to be international. Pitbull began his rap career in Miami only to find out his music appeals to southern states of America, which led to local success only. With his Spanish-speaking ability, Pitbull later began mixing English and Spanish verses in his rap music and this helped him gained international success in the industry that serves the English market and Spanish market simultaneously. Likewise, developing a British-American influence on my first rap album serves an international and meaningful purpose.

After I retire from my rap career in 2030, I truly believe an American and British documentary film director will create a documentary about my interesting rap career and about my meaningful journey from Miami to Paris to London. In this unpredictable world, most people would withdraw from a rap career if they began rapping at the age of 16 and not found success, yet patience and perseverance are two strings of success. As long as my rap music sells in the United Kingdom, United

**Christmas Story in Paris**                          **Luckner M. Pierre**

States, France and Canada, the international presence of my rap career will always make me truly happy and brings international success without stress. I am proud to be Mr. International and a symbol of international hope to people in Europe. I am international even in the future.

**Christmas Story in Paris**                   **Luckner M. Pierre**

### Well-being Needs True Happiness

"Less money with true happiness is more beneficial than more money without true happiness."

- **Mr. Pierre**

Money does not make me happy because money always gives me a false sense of security. I write books without a salary.

Indeed, I feel more confident and passionate in creative writing and in the element of storytelling in rap music as a hobby. While peacefulness is my creativity, creative writing alone alleviates internal and external stress, and I feel in touch with my real self.

Before January 2020, I never thought I could write and self-publish at least twelve short books in 2020 alone.

In storytelling descriptions, sharing certain moments of my life captures human imagination beyond human logic. Human logic cannot explain everything in life. For example, in my bilingual journey, many people are not aware that my French father does not speak English, yet learning the French language in France prepares me for the possibility of meeting my father for the first time if it ever happens.

Equally important, after learning Haitian Créole through active listening from my Haitian mother in her house in Miami, many people are not aware that even though I understand the Haitian Créole language in my heart, I am not able to read and write in Haitian Créole on paper because I completed all of my educational journey in Miami. Not in Haiti.

**Christmas Story in Paris**  Luckner M. Pierre

Overall, well-being will always need true happiness even if less money is earned.

**Christmas Story in Paris**  Luckner M. Pierre

### Christmas Loves Children
### by Mr. Pierre

Christmas trees
Christmas lights
Christmas breathes
Christmas kites

Christmas snows
in the city
where is Father Christmas?
no one knows

peppermint candy canes
to share
drink some ginger tea
feel cosy like a bear

Father Christmas
surrounded by children
glass of hot chocolate and mince pies
for every child on Christmas day

Christmas trees
Christmas lights
Christmas breathes
Christmas kites

Christmas Story in Paris                    Luckner M. Pierre

## Gratitude of Christmas
## by Mr. Pierre

turkey and sweet potatoes
next to sweet corn with mash potatoes
ready to serve

all eyes stare
at the juicy turkey
like a long curve

fulfil the prophecy of Christmas
in every country
everyone deserves

different gifts of Christmas
intuition on a mission
reaches far to be heard

praise and gratitude
refreshes the human soul
like a flying bird

Christmas belongs
to every country
like a herd

an attitude of gratitude
for Christmas
with more thankful words

Christmas Story in Paris                    Luckner M. Pierre

## Irrepressible Generosity
## by Mr. Pierre

generosity penetrates in my soul
living in my heart as a whole
with an attitude of gratitude

discourage by belittlement
yet my gratitude for generosity
is stronger than bitterness

though the world fails
to understand irrepressible generosity
generosity never fails

let me count all my blessings
without an end
I am proud to be generous from within

**Christmas Story in Paris**                          **Luckner M. Pierre**

## Life of a Volunteer
## by Mr. Pierre

volunteering turns my agony
into acts of joy
and in my heart fills the void

volunteering supersedes my bitterness
tickling my chest cavity
like a slice of pickle

volunteering is forever priceless
like money cannot buy
my emotional health

volunteering swims in my soul
restoring my well-being
to sustain my conscious

volunteering is my social life
my wife, my rights, my kite on the beach
and my future life

volunteering is my best friend
trusting me who blends
until the happiest end with faithful friends

volunteering prevails
investing thousands of hours in the community
life-changing moments to share

**Christmas Story in Paris**  Luckner M. Pierre

**BIO:**

Mr. Luckner Pierre is a French-born Haitian-American poet, prolific writer, rapper, storyteller, screenwriter, and a dedicated volunteer who highly values his heartfelt poems, hip hop songs and screenplays that speak to the human heart. While still a baby in French Guyana, his father abandoned him and forced his mother to move to Miami, Florida where he experienced physical abuse and racism.

Pierre is a graduate of Miami Central Senior High and Miami Dade College.

His favourite secular rapper is Tupac Shakur and his favourite non-secular rapper is Lecrae.

His favourite Tupac song is *"Mamma's Just A little Girl"* as this song encourages all men to appreciate the value of motherhood and that without women in this world no man would be born.

His favourite Lecrae song is *"I Did It for You"* as this song resonates in his heart as a powerful symbol of hope to alleviate global poverty.

His favourite poet is Pablo Neruda, who won the Nobel Prize for Literature in 1971.

In May 2018, Pierre self-published his inspirational book *"Volunteering is a Lifestyle: More Valuable than Money,"* as it relates to his five years of volunteer experience in Europe.

### Christmas Story in Paris                    Luckner M. Pierre

In March 2018, he self-published his poetry book, *"Courageous Life through Poetry."* Out of all the books he has written,

At the age of fifteen, Pierre's first job was cleaning the floor at a local supermarket. Because the labour laws in America do not permit teenagers to work, his manager kept him for only one week, yet Pierre appreciated the job because his father was not there to support him and his mother passed away when he was twelve years old.

His favourite teenage experience was when he took his half-sister to the day care centre in the mornings and brought her home in the afternoons after school while his single-parent mother was a bus driver working in the mornings and afternoons.

Pierre believes if he was raised in New York he would have gained acceptance in the New York society as opposed to the Miami society because New York has a reputation of diversity.

While London is still his favourite city, his favourite American city is New York because since the age of thirteen he cultivated the New York state of mind, and he fell in love with the lyrical content of famous New York rappers: *2Pac, Nas, Mobb Deep* and *Notorious B.I.G.*

In fact, his style of rapping is very similar to the typical New York rapper.

Though he loves the British accent with a passion, he will always cherish the New York lifestyle in his courageous heart. On the other hand, Pierre also loves country music as it appeals to his senses and he sees the vision of combining rap lyrics with a country instrumental beat.

**Christmas Story in Paris**                          **Luckner M. Pierre**

Since November 2017, Pierre has gained professional experience as Father Christmas.

## About the Author

Pierre earned an Associate in Arts degree from Miami Dade College.

His insightful thinking helped him awaken his senses and develop his spiritual intelligence to write literary books about his real-life experiences with realistic concepts to encourage and enlighten everyone in the world.

His intelligence and integrity has placed him in leadership roles where he can lead people to mentorship, academic success, community involvement and encourage people to break free from irrational cultural beliefs and love humanity. He is interested in anthropology, sociology, philanthropy, charitable activities and Christmas stories.

His humble goal is to become a philanthropist and a motivational speaker through encouragement. He is determined and destined to set a high standard of excellence in the music industry.

His books will continue to impress, inspire, and motivate others for generations to come.